NATURAL WONDERS
MARBLE CAVES OF PATAGONIA

by Katie Chanez

Ideas for Parents and Teachers

Pogo Books let children practice reading informational text while introducing them to nonfiction features such as headings, labels, sidebars, maps, and diagrams, as well as a table of contents, glossary, and index.

Carefully leveled text with a strong photo match offers early fluent readers the support they need to succeed.

Before Reading

- "Walk" through the book and point out the various nonfiction features. Ask the student what purpose each feature serves.
- Look at the glossary together. Read and discuss the words.

Read the Book

- Have the child read the book independently.
- Invite them to list questions that arise from reading.

After Reading

- Discuss the child's questions. Talk about how they might find answers to those questions.
- Prompt the child to think more. Ask: Did you know about the marble caves before reading this book? What more would you like to learn about them?

Pogo Books are published by Jump!
5357 Penn Avenue South
Minneapolis, MN 55419
www.jumplibrary.com

Copyright © 2025 Jump!
International copyright reserved in all countries.
No part of this book may be reproduced in any form without written permission from the publisher.

Library of Congress Cataloging-in-Publication Data

Names: Chanez, Katie, author.
Title: Marble caves of Patagonia / by Katie Chanez.
Description: Minneapolis, MN: Jump!, Inc., [2025]
Series: Natural wonders | Includes index.
Audience: Ages 7-10
Identifiers: LCCN 2024035261 (print)
LCCN 2024035262 (ebook)
ISBN 9798892135467 (hardcover)
ISBN 9798892135474 (paperback)
ISBN 9798892135481 (ebook)
Subjects: LCSH: Caves—Patagonia (Argentina and Chile)—Juvenile literature.
Classification: LCC GB608.34 .C53 2025 (print)
LCC GB608.34 (ebook)
DDC 551.44/709827—dc23/eng/20240909
LC record available at https://lccn.loc.gov/2024035261
LC ebook record available at https://lccn.loc.gov/2024035262

Editor: Alyssa Sorenson
Designer: Molly Ballanger

Photo Credits: Alberto Loyo/Shutterstock, cover; JHVEPhoto/Shutterstock, 1; Alejandro Girela/Shutterstock, 3; Andreas Werth/Alamy, 4; Prosto Maestro/Shutterstock, 5; Naeblys/iStock, 6-7; Galyna Andrushko/Shutterstock, 8; M9K/Shutterstock, 9; Freedom_wanted/Shutterstock, 10-11; Naeblys/Shutterstock, 12-13; Galyna Andrushko/Dreamstime, 14-15; San Hoyano/Shutterstock, 16-17; Guaxinim/Shutterstock, 18; Raquel Mogado/Alamy, 19; maxcavalera/Stockimo/Alamy, 20-21; Shruthi Govardhan/Shutterstock, 23.

Printed in the United States of America at Corporate Graphics in North Mankato, Minnesota.

TABLE OF CONTENTS

CHAPTER 1
Colorful Caves 4

CHAPTER 2
How They Formed 8

CHAPTER 3
Visiting the Caves 18

QUICK FACTS & TOOLS
At a Glance 22
Glossary 23
Index 24
To Learn More 24

CHAPTER 1
COLORFUL CAVES

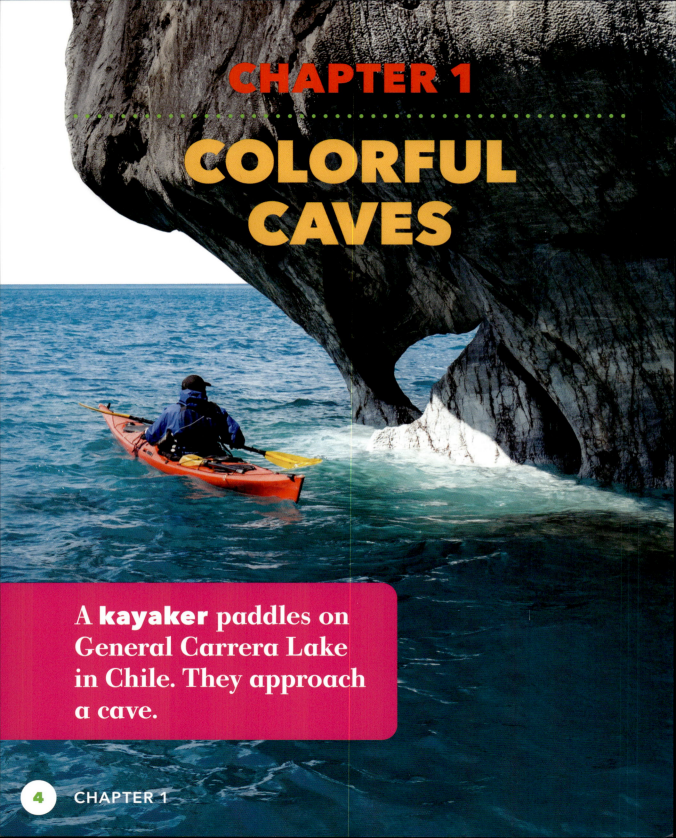

A **kayaker** paddles on General Carrera Lake in Chile. They approach a cave.

The kayaker enters. The cave walls look blue! What is this beautiful place? It is a marble cave.

CHAPTER 1

The marble caves are in Patagonia. This area covers the southern tip of South America. It includes parts of Chile and Argentina.

WHAT DO YOU THINK?

The caves are in Chile's Capillas de Mármol. This is a **natural sanctuary**. Have you ever been to a place that protects nature? Do you think there should be more of them? Why or why not?

CHAPTER 2
HOW THEY FORMED

The caves took millions of years to form. It all started between 400 and 200 million years ago. A **shallow** sea was here then.

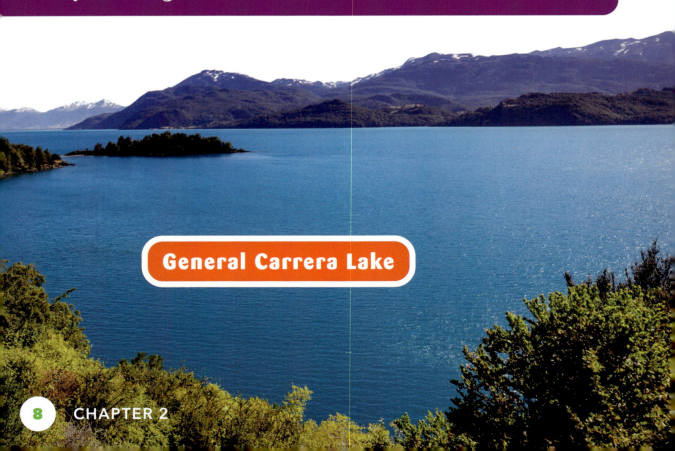

General Carrera Lake

Animals lived in the sea. When they died, they sank. Hard parts like bones and shells built up at the bottom. **Pressure** pushed down on them. Bottom **layers** hardened into limestone.

limestone

CHAPTER 2
9

Earth's **tectonic plates** moved. This buried the limestone deep in Earth. Pressure and heat from Earth's **core** changed the limestone. It turned into marble. The plates moved more. They lifted the marble closer to the surface.

marble

TAKE A LOOK!

How do tectonic plates move? Take a look!

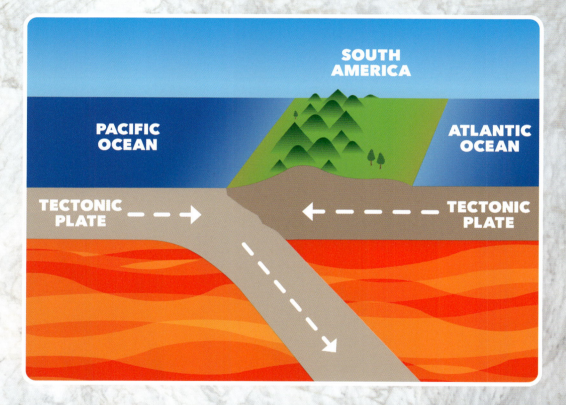

CHAPTER 2

The Andes Mountains run through Patagonia. The mountains have snow, ice, and **glaciers** on them. A glacier created General Carrera Lake. How? Its weight caused it to slide down the mountain. This **eroded** the soil. The glacier **carved** where the lake is.

CHAPTER 2

Glaciers melted. Water flowed down the mountains. It filled the lake. Around 6,200 years ago, waves of lake water crashed against the marble. Over time, they eroded part of the marble. The caves formed!

14 CHAPTER 2

TAKE A LOOK!

How did the marble caves form? Take a look!

① Limestone formed and was buried.

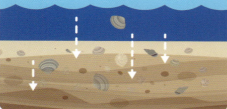

② Heat and pressure turned the limestone to marble.

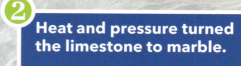

③ Tectonic plates moved. The marble rose to Earth's surface.

④ Lake waves eroded the marble. Caves formed.

CHAPTER 2 15

The walls of the caves often look blue. Why? **Silt** in the lake makes the water look turquoise. The cave walls **reflect** the color of the water.

DID YOU KNOW?

The caves do not always look the same. The **water level** changes throughout the year. This affects how much light is reflected. The caves look bluer when the water level is higher!

CHAPTER 2

CHAPTER 2

CHAPTER 3

VISITING THE CAVES

The caves are not easy to reach. Only one road connects much of Patagonia to the rest of Chile.

The caves are in the middle of the lake. People cannot walk or drive to them. They can only get to them by boat. Kayaks and boat tours are popular ways to see the caves.

CHAPTER 3

During parts of the year, the water is low enough for boats to go inside the caves. People enjoy the colors inside.

The lake's water continues to erode the marble. This means the caves are always changing!

WHAT DO YOU THINK?

Many people travel to see the caves. Would you like to visit? Why or why not?

CHAPTER 3

QUICK FACTS & TOOLS

AT A GLANCE

MARBLE CAVES

Location:
Chilean Patagonia

Date Formed:
about 6,200 years ago

How They Formed:
water eroded layers of rock

Number of Yearly Visitors:
thousands of people

GLOSSARY

carved: Cut wood, stone, or another hard substance.

core: The intensely hot, most inner part of Earth.

eroded: Wore away with water, wind, heat, or ice.

glaciers: Slow-moving masses of ice in mountains or polar regions that form when snow does not melt.

kayaker: Someone traveling in a kayak, a small, light boat rowed by a double-sided paddle.

layers: Parts of something that lie over or under other parts.

natural sanctuary: An area of land set aside to protect plants and animals.

pressure: The force produced by pressing on something.

reflect: To throw back light from a surface.

shallow: Not deep.

silt: Fine particles of soil that are carried by water and eventually settle on the bottom of a river or lake.

tectonic plates: Large, flat sheets of rock that make up Earth's crust.

water level: The average height of a body of water.

QUICK FACTS & TOOLS

INDEX

Andes Mountains 12, 14
animals 9
Argentina 7
Capillas de Mármol 7
Chile 4, 7, 18
color 16, 20
eroded 12, 14, 15, 20
General Carrera Lake 4, 12, 14, 15, 16, 19, 20
glaciers 12, 14

heat 10, 15
kayaker 4, 5, 19
limestone 9, 10, 15
marble 5, 7, 10, 14, 15, 20
natural sanctuary 7
Patagonia 7, 12, 18
pressure 9, 10, 15
silt 16
tectonic plates 10, 11, 15

TO LEARN MORE

Finding more information is as easy as 1, 2, 3.

❶ **Go to www.factsurfer.com**
❷ **Enter "marblecavesofPatagonia" into the search box.**
❸ **Choose your book to see a list of websites.**

24 QUICK FACTS & TOOLS